Level A · Book 2

**QuickReads®**
A Research-Based Fluency Program

Elfrieda H. Hiebert, Ph.D.

MODERN CURRICULUM PRESS

Pearson Learning Group

## Program Reviewers and Consultants

**Dr. Barbara A. Baird**
Director of Federal Programs/Richardson ISD
Richardson, TX

**Dr. Kate Kinsella**
Dept. of Secondary Education and Step to College Program
San Francisco State University
San Francisco, CA

**Pat Sears**
Early Child Coordinator/Virginia Beach Public Schools
Virginia Beach, VA

**Dr. Judith B. Smith**
Supervisor of ESOL and World and Classical Languages/Baltimore City Public Schools
Baltimore, MD

The following people have contributed to the development of this product:

Art and Design: Denise Ingrassia, David Mager, Judy Mahoney,
   Salita Mehta, Elbaliz Mendez, Dan Thomas, Dan Trush

Editorial: Lynn W. Kloss

Inventory: Levon Carter

Marketing: Alison Bruno

Production/Manufacturing: Lorraine Allen, Carlos Blas, Leslie Greenberg

Publishing Operations: Jennifer Van Der Heide

ISBN 0-7652-6720-9

Printed in the United States of America

7  8  9  10      08  07

1-800-321-3106
www.pearsonlearning.com

# Contents

SCIENCE **How Things Are Measured**

Measuring Earth . . . . . . . . . . . . . . . . . . . . . . .10

Tools for Measuring . . . . . . . . . . . . . . . . . . . .12

Using a Ruler . . . . . . . . . . . . . . . . . . . . . . . .14

Long, Wide, and High . . . . . . . . . . . . . . . . . .16

Time . . . . . . . . . . . . . . . . . . . . . . . . . . . . . .18

**How Things Are Measured Review** . . . . . . .20

 Connect Your Ideas . . . . . . . . . . . . . . . . . . .23

# Contents

SCIENCE **Seasons**

Earth's Tilt . . . . . . . . . . . . . . . . . . . . . . . . . . . .24

Spring . . . . . . . . . . . . . . . . . . . . . . . . . . . . . . . .26

Summer . . . . . . . . . . . . . . . . . . . . . . . . . . . . . . .28

Fall . . . . . . . . . . . . . . . . . . . . . . . . . . . . . . .30

Winter . . . . . . . . . . . . . . . . . . . . . . . . . . . . . . .32

**Seasons Review** . . . . . . . . . . . . . . . . . . . . . . .34

 Connect Your Ideas . . . . . . . . . . . . . . . . . .37

SCIENCE  # Stars

What Is a Star? . . . . . . . . . . . . . . . . . . . . . . .38

Stars of Different Colors . . . . . . . . . . . . . . . .40

Stars at Night . . . . . . . . . . . . . . . . . . . . . . . .42

Star Patterns . . . . . . . . . . . . . . . . . . . . . . . .44

Shooting Stars . . . . . . . . . . . . . . . . . . . . . . .46

**Stars Review** . . . . . . . . . . . . . . . . . . . . . . . .48

Connect Your Ideas . . . . . . . . . . . . . . . . . .51

# Contents

SOCIAL STUDIES

## Houses Around the World

What Is a House? . . . . . . . . . . . . . . . . . . . . . .52

Houses of Ice . . . . . . . . . . . . . . . . . . . . . . . .54

Houses on Stilts . . . . . . . . . . . . . . . . . . . . . .56

Houses on the Go . . . . . . . . . . . . . . . . . . . . .58

Houses in the City . . . . . . . . . . . . . . . . . . . . .60

**Houses Around the World Review** . . . . . . . .62

Connect Your Ideas . . . . . . . . . . . . . . . . . . .65

SOCIAL
STUDIES

# Places People Work

Outdoor Jobs . . . . . . . . . . . . . . . . . . . . . . . . . . . . .66

Office Jobs . . . . . . . . . . . . . . . . . . . . . . . . . . . . . .68

Store Jobs . . . . . . . . . . . . . . . . . . . . . . . . . . . . . .70

Travel Jobs . . . . . . . . . . . . . . . . . . . . . . . . . . . . . .72

Jobs at Home . . . . . . . . . . . . . . . . . . . . . . . . . . . . .74

**Places People Work Review** . . . . . . . . . . . . . .76

 Connect Your Ideas . . . . . . . . . . . . . . . . . . . .79

# Contents

SOCIAL STUDIES

## Lakes and Ponds

What Are Lakes and Ponds? . . . . . . . . . . . . . . . .80

Kinds of Lakes . . . . . . . . . . . . . . . . . . . . . . . .82

Life in Lakes and Ponds . . . . . . . . . . . . . . . . .84

Part-Time Ponds . . . . . . . . . . . . . . . . . . . . . .86

Fun at Lakes and Ponds . . . . . . . . . . . . . . . . .88

**Lakes and Ponds Review** . . . . . . . . . . . . . . . .90

 Connect Your Ideas . . . . . . . . . . . . . . . . . .93

Reading Log . . . . . . . . . . . . . . . . . . . . . . . . . .94

Self-Check Graph . . . . . . . . . . . . . . . . . . . . . .96

# Acknowledgments

All photography © Pearson Education, Inc. (PEI) unless otherwise specifically noted.

Cover: © Superstock. 3: Steve Shott/DK Images. 4: Stouffer Productions/Animals Animals/Earth Scenes. 5: © David Lawrence/Corbis. 6: Jeff Schultz/Alaska Stock Images/PictureQuest. 7: © Michael Newman/PhotoEdit/PictureQuest. 8: Doug Wechsler/ Animals Animals/Earth Scenes. 10: © Myrleen Ferguson Cate/PhotoEdit. 12: Steve Shott/DK Images. 16–18: © David Young-Wolff/PhotoEdit. 24: © Michael Newman/PhotoEdit. 26: © Darren Bennett/Animals Animals/Earth Scenes. 28: © Tom Brakefield/Corbis. 30: © Dominique Braud/Animals Animals/Earth Scenes. 32: Stouffer Productions/Animals Animals/Earth Scenes. 38: © David Lawrence/ Corbis. 40: Fred Whitehead/Animals Animals/Earth Scenes. 42: Bill Brooks/Masterfile. 46: © Jonathan Blair/Corbis. 52: © Neil Rabinowitz/ Corbis. 54: Jeff Schultz/Alaska Stock Images/PictureQuest. 56: Jeff Greenberg/PhotoEdit/PictureQuest. 58: © Wolfgang Kaehler/Corbis. 60: © Erik Freeland/Corbis. 66: David R. Frazier/David R. Frazier Photography. 68: Phyllis Picardi/Stock Boston, Inc/PictureQuest. 70: © Don Mason/Corbis. 72: © Tony Freeman/PhotoEdit. 74: © Michael Newman/PhotoEdit/PictureQuest. 80: © Johnny Johnson/Animals Animals/Earth Scenes. 82: © Scott T. Smith/Corbis. 84: Doug Wechsler/Animals Animals/Earth Scenes. 86: E.R. Degginger/Bruce Coleman, Inc. 88: © Robert Brenner/PhotoEdit.

# How Things Are Measured

How many things in this
picture can be measured?

# Measuring Earth

Words like *big* or *round* are used to talk about Earth. Beach balls can also be big and round. Of course, beach balls[25] are not as big as Earth. To learn how much bigger Earth is than a beach ball, you can measure the sizes of both Earth[50] and the beach ball.

Many things on Earth can be measured. Beach balls can be measured to find out how big around they are. Their[75] weight can also be measured. How far people throw beach balls can be measured, too.[90]

# How Things Are Measured

This scale shows how much the cat weighs.

# Tools for Measuring

People can put their arms around things like beach balls to measure them. However, one person may have longer arms than another[25] person. If their arms are different sizes, people will measure things differently. That's why people use tools to measure things.

Rulers with inches, feet, and[50] yards are used to measure how long, wide, and high things are. Clocks with minutes and hours are used to measure time. Things are also[75] weighed to measure how many pounds they are. Tools can show people how big things really are.[92]

# How Things Are Measured

These boys are using a ruler to measure how high the board is.

# Using a Ruler

In the United States, people use rulers with inches, feet, and yards to find out how long, wide, or high things are.[25] All rulers in the United States use the same scale for inches, feet, and yards. An inch is the same on every ruler. If you[50] put two rulers together, the inches always line up.

Many countries measure things with the metric scale. Some rulers in the United States use both[75] scales. These rulers have inches on one side and the metric scale on the other side.[91]

# How Things Are Measured

Measuring things can help people
find a box that will fit them.

# Long, Wide, and High

Someone is looking for a box to mail a book. To get the right box, the person must know three things[25] about the box and the book.

First, the person must measure the book and the box with a ruler to see how long they are.[50] Next, both need to be measured to see how wide they are. Last, both need to be measured to see how high they are. If[75] the book is bigger than the box in any of these three ways, the person must find another box.[94]

# How Things Are Measured

Clocks help people measure
minutes and hours.

# Time

Rulers can measure the size of books and boxes. However, to measure a person's age or the day of the week, you need tools[25] that tell time.

Clocks can measure short blocks of time, like minutes and hours. Calendars can measure longer blocks of time, like days, months, and[50] years.

Calendars are based on how long it takes Earth to go around the Sun. Earth goes around the Sun once every year. That means[75] that a person who is eight years old has made eight trips around the Sun.[90]

# How Things Are Measured

Write words that will help you remember what you learned.

## Measuring Earth

_____

_____

_____

## Tools for Measuring

_____

_____

_____

## Using a Ruler

_____

_____

_____

## Long, Wide, and High

_____

_____

_____

## Time

_____

_____

_____

## Measuring Earth

**1**. How can you find out the size of a beach ball?

   Ⓐ by measuring the beach ball

   Ⓑ by measuring Earth

   Ⓒ by looking at other beach balls

**2**. Name two things you can learn by measuring something.

_____

_____

_____

## Tools for Measuring

**1**. This reading is MAINLY about ___

   Ⓐ why we use clocks to measure time.

   Ⓑ the size of a person's arms.

   Ⓒ why we use tools to measure things.

**2**. Why do we use tools for measuring?

_____

_____

_____

# How Things Are Measured

## Using a Ruler

1. Rulers can measure ___

   Ⓐ how long things are.

   Ⓑ how much things cost.

   Ⓒ how much things weigh.

2. Why should an inch be the same on every ruler?

_____

_____

_____


## Long, Wide, and High

1. Why would a person measure a book before finding a box for it?

   Ⓐ so the person can use the right ruler

   Ⓑ so the book will fit inside the box

   Ⓒ so the book will be bigger than the box

2. What three things must a person know to get a box for a book?

_____

_____

_____

## Time

**1.** This reading is MAINLY about ___

Ⓐ how to measure time.

Ⓑ how to use clocks and calendars.

Ⓒ how to measure Earth.

**2.** Tell about two tools that measure time.

_____

_____

_____

## Connect Your Ideas

**1.** Tell about two tools people use to measure things.

_____

_____

_____

**2.** How would you show a person how to measure something?

_____

_____

_____

This globe shows how Earth is tilted in space.

# Earth's Tilt

Think of Earth as being on a pole that tilts to one side. Earth isn't really on a pole. However, it is tilted[25] so that some parts of Earth are closer to the Sun than other parts. When a part of Earth is closer to the Sun, the[50] Sun is in the sky longer and it is warmer there.

Earth also moves around the Sun. Earth's movement and its tilt mean that the[75] parts of Earth that are closest to the Sun change over a year. These changes make the different seasons.[94]

Spring is the time when
many birds have their babies.

# Spring

The United States is in North America. The first day of spring in North America is March 20 or 21. On this day, North[25] America has 12 hours of day and 12 hours of night. After the first day of spring, the part of Earth that has North America[50] begins to tilt closer to the Sun. This means that the Sun is in the sky a little longer every day until summer starts.

In[75] spring, the Sun's warmth helps plants begin to grow. Many animals, like birds, have babies in spring, too.[93]

Summer is the time when baby
animals learn to live on their own.

# Summer

In North America, summer begins on June 20, 21, or 22. This day is the longest of the year. On this day, Earth is[25] tilted so that North America is close to the Sun. The Sun is in the sky for almost 15 hours. After the first day of[50] summer, North America begins to tilt away from the Sun a little more each day.

The long summer days give plants the sunlight they need[75] to grow. Baby animals, like birds, also learn how to get food and live on their own in summer.[94]

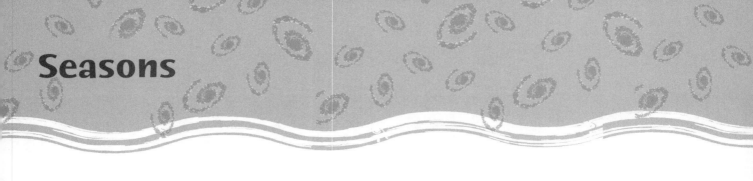

Fall is the time when animals get set for winter.

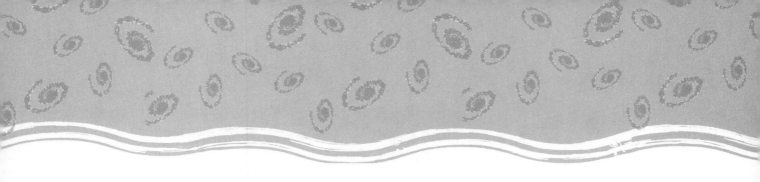

# Fall

As in spring, fall begins on a day that has 12 hours of day and 12 hours of night. In North America, the first[25] day of fall is September 22 or 23. After this September day, the part of Earth that has North America begins to tilt away from[50] the Sun. This means that each day in fall has less sunlight.

Fall is the season when plants and animals get set for winter. The[75] leaves on many plants and trees fall off. Some birds also fly to warmer places to find food.[93]

# Seasons

In winter, bears go to sleep
until spring comes again.

# Winter

In North America, winter begins on December 21 or 22. This is the shortest day of the year. On this December day, Earth is[25] tilted so that North America is far from the Sun. The Sun is in the sky for only nine hours. After the first day of[50] winter, North America begins to tilt toward the Sun again.

The shorter days of winter give plants and animals less sunlight for warmth and growth.[75] Birds that have gone to warm places stay there. Some animals, like bears, sleep until spring comes again.[93]

 **Seasons**

Write words that will help you remember what you learned.

### Earth's Tilt

_____

_____

_____

_____

### Spring

_____

_____

_____

_____

### Summer

_____

_____

_____

_____

### Fall

_____

_____

_____

_____

### Winter

_____

_____

_____

_____

## Earth's Tilt

1. "Earth's Tilt" is MAINLY about ___

    Ⓐ why Earth is warm all year.

    Ⓑ what happens because Earth tilts.

    Ⓒ how the Sun tilts toward Earth.

2. How does Earth's tilt make some parts of Earth warmer?

_____

_____

_____

## Spring

1. What happens on the first day of spring in North America?

    Ⓐ Earth tilts away from the Sun.

    Ⓑ Day and night are both 12 hours long.

    Ⓒ The Sun shines on the United States.

2. What happens to plants and animals in spring?

_____

_____

_____

**Seasons**

## Summer

**1.** On the first day of summer, North America is ___

   Ⓐ close to the Sun.

   Ⓑ far away from the Sun.

   Ⓒ tilting toward Earth.

**2.** Why is summer good for plants and animals?

_____

_____

_____

## Fall

**1.** In fall, Earth tilts so that North America has ___

   Ⓐ less sunlight each day.

   Ⓑ more sunlight each day.

   Ⓒ more days in fall.

**2.** What do plants and animals do in fall?

_____

_____

_____

## Winter

**1**. In winter, Earth tilts so that North America ___

    Ⓐ is close to the Sun.

    Ⓑ has lots of sunlight.

    Ⓒ is far from the Sun.

**2**. What do animals do in winter?

_____

_____

_____

## Connect Your Ideas

**1**. Tell how animals' lives are different in summer and in winter.

_____

_____

_____

**2**. How does Earth's tilt make the seasons?

_____

_____

_____

# Stars

In this picture, stars are all
around Earth and the Moon.

# What Is a Star?

When the Sun sets and the sky gets dark, stars can be seen in the night sky. Stars are large balls[25] of gas in space. The gas that makes up stars gives off heat and light. This heat and light is the same as the heat[50] and light that the Sun gives off. That is because the Sun is a star.

Stars are much larger than Earth. For example, the Sun[75] is 100 times larger than Earth. In space, there are many stars even larger than the Sun.[92]

# Stars

The Sun looks yellow because
it is between old and new.

# Stars of Different Colors

All stars give off heat and light. Stars of different ages give off different amounts of heat and light. The different[25] amounts of heat and light make stars different colors.

New stars give off the most heat and light. These stars are the color blue. Old[50] stars give off little heat and light. These stars are the color red. Stars that are between old and new are other colors, like yellow.[75] The Sun, which is a star that is between old and new, is the color yellow.[91]

# Stars

To see lots of stars, people must
be far away from city lights.

# Stars at Night

Because the Sun is the nearest star to Earth, it blocks the light of other stars during the day. At night, people[25] can see many of these other stars. On clear and dark nights in North America, some stars can always be seen. One of these stars[50] is the North Pole Star.

To see large numbers of stars, people have to be far from the bright lights of cities. On dark and[75] clear nights in places far from cities, people can see as many as 2,000 stars.[90]

# Stars

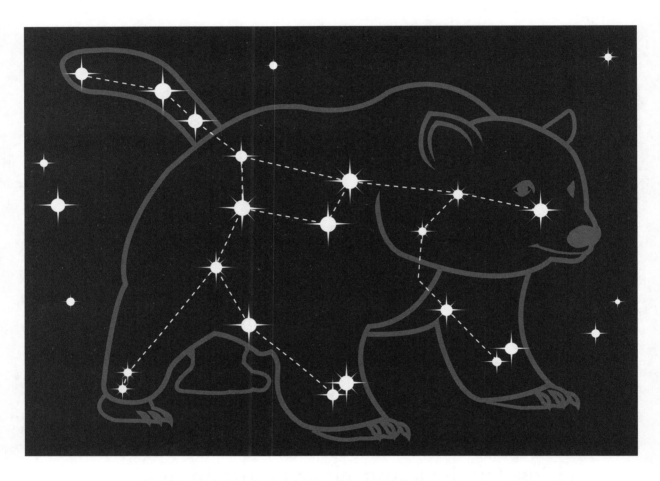

This drawing shows the star pattern called the Great Bear.

# Star Patterns

Long ago, people made patterns out of the stars in the night sky. One star pattern looked like a great bear. Another star[25] pattern looked like a little bear.

People began to tell stories about the star patterns they saw. They told these stories to their children. Their[50] children later told the stories to their own children.

Many of the names that people of long ago gave to these star patterns are still[75] used today. One star pattern is called the Great Bear. Another star pattern is called the Little Bear.[93]

# Stars

This picture shows lots of shooting
stars falling into the air around Earth.

# Shooting Stars

Sometimes, it looks like a star is falling very fast in the night sky. People call this a shooting star. However, shooting stars[25] are not stars at all.

What people call a shooting star is really a rock in space that is falling toward Earth. The white line[50] that people see is the space rock as it burns up in the air around Earth. These space rocks can be as small as dust[75] or as big as a car. Some people have found space rocks that have hit Earth.[91]

Write words that will help you remember what you learned.

### What Is a Star?

_____

_____

_____

_____

### Stars of Different Colors

_____

_____

_____

_____

### Stars at Night

_____

_____

_____

_____

### Star Patterns

_____

_____

_____

_____

### Shooting Stars

_____

_____

_____

_____

## What Is a Star?

**1.** What is the Sun?

    Ⓐ a ball of stars

    Ⓑ a ball like Earth

    Ⓒ a star

**2.** What is a star?

_____

_____

_____

## Stars of Different Colors

**1.** "Stars of Different Colors" is MAINLY about ___

    Ⓐ why we see stars at night.

    Ⓑ why stars are different colors.

    Ⓒ why stars are different ages.

**2.** Why are stars different colors?

_____

_____

_____

 **Stars**

## Stars at Night

**1.** We see stars at night because the Sun ___

   Ⓐ is far away from Earth.

   Ⓑ is close to the North Pole Star.

   Ⓒ is not blocking the stars' light.

**2.** Why can't people see large numbers of stars in the city at night?

_____

_____

_____

## Star Patterns

**1.** Another good name for "Star Patterns" is ___

   Ⓐ "Why We See Stars."

   Ⓑ "Stars That Have Bears."

   Ⓒ "Stories About Stars."

**2.** What is a star pattern?

_____

_____

_____

## Shooting Stars

1. Shooting stars are really ___

   Ⓐ rocks that have hit Earth.

   Ⓑ space rocks falling toward Earth.

   Ⓒ stars that shoot around in the sky.

2. What is the white line in a shooting star?

   _____

   _____

   _____

## Connect Your Ideas

1. What are two facts about stars you learned in these readings?

   _____

   _____

   _____

2. Suppose there was another reading. Would it be about how hot stars are or about rocks on Earth? Why?

   _____

   _____

   _____

# Houses Around the World

How do these houses look different
from the houses in your town?

# What Is a House?

Houses are places where people live. Houses can be made in many sizes. Some houses have one room. Others have many[25] rooms. Some houses are made for many families. Other houses are made for only one family.

Houses also can be made from different things. Most[50] often, some or all of a house is made of wood. However, houses can also be made of stone, brick, mud, leaves, straw, and even[75] snow. Around the world, people often make houses from things that are found near where they want to live.[94]

# Houses Around the World

This girl and her igloo are near the North Pole.

# Houses of Ice

Few trees grow on the icy land near the North Pole. In addition, stones are hard to get loose. With little wood[25] and few stones, people in the North made houses from what they had—snow. Houses made from blocks of snow are called igloos. Although igloos[50] are made of snow, they are warm inside. This is because people inside igloos make fires and stay close together.

Today near the North Pole,[75] planes and ships bring things used to build houses. However, some people still build igloos when they hunt animals.[94]

# Houses Around the World

The stilts under this house
help it stay dry.

# Houses on Stilts

A stilt is a tall pole that is often made of wood. Houses built on stilts sit high above the ground. Living [25] high above the ground is useful sometimes. It is useful to have a house on stilts when there are many bugs on the ground that [50] bite people.

Houses on stilts are also useful when people live near the water. Rivers and lakes can change in size. When rivers and lakes [75] rise, water flows under houses on stilts. In this way, the houses and the people inside them stay dry. [94]

# Houses Around the World

These houses can be taken down
and moved to new places.

# Houses on the Go

Several groups of people live in one place for only a few months at a time. When their animals eat all[25] of the food in a place, the people move to a place that has more food. One of these groups lives in China.

All of[50] the groups that move from place to place have houses that are easy to put together. These houses are also easy to take apart. The[75] people in China who move around build their houses using thin, light poles and animal skins.[91]

# Houses Around the World

Many people can live in
these apartment buildings.

# Houses in the City

In cities where there isn't much space, huge houses are built that hold many people. Each person or family has its[25] own part of the huge house. However, the home of each person or family is apart from the others. That's why each home inside these[50] huge buildings is called an apartment. The huge houses are called apartment buildings.

Some apartments have many rooms, while others have just a few rooms.[75] Apartment buildings give homes to many people in the city without using too much land.[90]

Write words that will help you remember what you learned.

### What Is a House?

_____

_____

_____

### Houses of Ice

_____

_____

_____

### Houses on Stilts

_____

_____

_____

### Houses on the Go

_____

_____

_____

### Houses in the City

_____

_____

_____

_____

## What Is a House?

**1.** Another good name for "What Is a House?" is ___

   Ⓐ "Houses With Many Rooms."

   Ⓑ "Stone and Wood Houses."

   Ⓒ "Different Kinds of Houses."

**2.** What are two things you learned about houses in this reading?

_____

_____

_____

## Houses of Ice

**1.** What is one thing that makes igloos warm?

   Ⓐ It is warm at the North Pole.

   Ⓑ The wood in igloos keeps people warm.

   Ⓒ People inside igloos stay close together.

**2.** Why do people near the North Pole build igloos?

_____

_____

_____

**Houses Around the World**

## Houses on Stilts

**1.** What is a stilt?

Ⓐ a river

Ⓑ a house

Ⓒ a tall pole

**2.** What is one reason people build houses on stilts?

_____

_____

_____

## Houses on the Go

**1.** Why do the people in this reading move from place to place?

Ⓐ to find homes for their families

Ⓑ to find food for their animals

Ⓒ to find homes for their animals

**2.** Tell about the houses of people who move from place to place.

_____

_____

_____

## Houses in the City

**1.** "Houses in the City" is MAINLY about ___

Ⓐ how to build apartments.

Ⓑ buildings where many people live.

Ⓒ houses that use a lot of land.

**2.** What is an apartment building?

_____

_____

_____

## Connect Your Ideas

**1.** Tell about two different kinds of houses.

_____

_____

_____

**2.** How are all houses alike?

_____

_____

_____

# Places People Work

Farming is a job that people do outdoors.

# Outdoor Jobs

Some people do their job outdoors. Farmers who grow plants like corn or wheat spend most of their time outside. Farmers who take[25] care of animals like cows or pigs also work outside most of the time. People who take care of parks or who cut down trees[50] work outside, too. In cities, people who fight fires and crime also spend much of their time outdoors.

People who work outdoors are outside when[75] it is warm and sunny. However, they also work outside when it rains or is cold.[91]

# Places People Work

These doctors are helping someone get well.

# Office Jobs

There are many kinds of offices. However, most people who work in offices spend their time inside. One kind of office is a[25] bank. People keep their money in banks. Another kind of office is a doctor's office. People go to doctors' offices when they are sick.

People[50] who work in offices often work in teams. In banks, teams keep the money safe. In doctors' offices, teams make sure that sick people get[75] the help they need. In offices, everyone on a team works together to get the job done.[92]

# Places People Work

People who work in stores must know about the things they sell.

# Store Jobs

Some people sell things from carts outdoors. However, most people who sell things work inside stores. People with store jobs should be kind[25] to those who want to buy things. This is because people won't buy things in stores where workers are not kind.

People who work in[50] stores also must know about the things they sell. Some stores sell only a few things. Other stores sell many things. People who work in[75] stores must know where to find things, how things work, and how much things cost.[90]

# Places People Work

People who drive buses travel
when they do their job.

# Travel Jobs

In some jobs, people travel from place to place. People who drive buses, trains, and planes travel when they do their job. Some[25] people sell things in different cities. They travel to get their job done, too. People who fight for our country also have to travel. Sometimes[50] these people are gone from home for a long time.

When people travel while they do their job, they get to see new places and[75] meet new people. However, people who travel are also gone from home much of the time.[91]

# Places People Work

Writing music is a job that
people can do at home.

# Jobs at Home

In some jobs, people work at home. People bake cakes in their home to sell. People also take care of children in[25] their home.

Many artists make their pictures at home. Many writers write their stories at home, too. Most artists and writers don't need other people[50] to help them make their pictures or stories. However, many do need people outside their home to sell their pictures or stories. When people work[75] at home, they don't have to travel to go to their job. They can work anywhere they wish.[93]

# Places People Work

Write words that will help you remember what you learned.

### Outdoor Jobs

### Office Jobs

### Store Jobs

### Travel Jobs

### Jobs at Home

## Outdoor Jobs

**1.** What is the main idea of this reading?

Ⓐ Farming is an outdoor job.

Ⓑ Farmers grow plants.

Ⓒ Some people work outdoors.

**2.** What are two outdoor jobs you learned about in this reading?

_____

_____

_____

## Office Jobs

**1.** Two kinds of offices are ___

Ⓐ banks and doctors' offices.

Ⓑ doctors' offices and farms.

Ⓒ fire fighting and banks.

**2.** How do you think working in teams helps people do their job?

_____

_____

_____

**Places People Work**

## Store Jobs

**1.** "Store Jobs" is MAINLY about ___

Ⓐ how to buy things in a store.

Ⓑ what store workers do.

Ⓒ why people build stores.

**2.** What are two things store workers must know about the things they sell?

_____

_____

_____

## Travel Jobs

**1.** In which two jobs do people often travel?

Ⓐ park jobs and bank jobs

Ⓑ store jobs and farm jobs

Ⓒ driving jobs and some selling jobs

**2.** Why might a person like having a travel job?

_____

_____

_____

## Jobs at Home

**1**. Which two jobs can people do at home?

   Ⓐ bake cakes and write stories

   Ⓑ work in a store and make pictures

   Ⓒ care for children and fight fires

**2**. Why do you think some people might like to work at home?

_____

_____

_____

## Connect Your Ideas

**1**. Choose two jobs you read about. Tell how they are the same.

_____

_____

_____

**2**. Choose two jobs you read about. Tell how they are different.

_____

_____

_____

# Lakes and Ponds

Some lakes are small enough so
that you can see the other side.

# What Are Lakes and Ponds?

Lakes and ponds are almost the same. Both are pools of water that have land around them. However, lakes are [25] bigger than ponds. Although some lakes, like the Great Lakes, are big, no lakes are as big as an ocean.

Lakes and ponds can change [50] in size over a year. They can also change in size from year to year. Lakes and ponds can even dry up and be gone [75] forever. This can take place when the water that feeds the lakes and ponds no longer runs into them. [94]

# Lakes and Ponds

Salt covers the rocks at this salt-water lake.

# Kinds of Lakes

Lakes that were part of oceans long ago have salt water. Some salt-water lakes are far from oceans. Some are even[25] in the middle of countries. Although the ocean has been gone for many years, these lakes still have salt water.

Other lakes were made long[50] ago when large blocks of ice moved over the land. The water in these lakes is fresh, not salty. Fresh-water lakes also form when[75] people make dams. People, animals, and plants all need the fresh water from lakes to stay alive.[92]

# Lakes and Ponds

Frogs and other animals live among
the plants near ponds.

# Life in Lakes and Ponds

Lakes and ponds are home to many plants and animals. Some plants and animals are too small to be seen[25] by people. The fish and bugs that live in or near lakes and ponds eat these small plants and animals.

The fish and bugs are[50] also food for other animals, like birds. Many birds go on long trips to warm places in the fall and come back in the spring.[75] Birds find some of the food they need in lakes and ponds to make these long trips.[92]

# Lakes and Ponds

Some of these tadpoles are still inside their eggs.

# Part-Time Ponds

Some ponds only last for part of a year. After the snow melts in spring, a hole in the ground fills with[25] water. This new pond gives animals like frogs the water they need to lay eggs.

By the middle of summer, much of the water in[50] the pond has gone. The eggs have become tadpoles, and the tadpoles have become frogs. The young frogs live on the land where the ponds[75] were. These places stay wet enough to have many bugs for the frogs to eat.[90]

# Lakes and Ponds

People can have fun at lakes and
ponds by riding in boats.

# Fun at Lakes and Ponds

Many people go to lakes and ponds to have fun. Some people go to see and hear the birds that[25] live close to lakes and ponds. Other people like to draw or take pictures of the plants and animals that live near lakes and ponds.[50]

When it is hot in summer, people also like to swim or cool off in lakes and ponds. Sometimes, they go to lakes and ponds[75] to catch fish to eat. People even use boats to ride on some lakes and ponds.[91]

**Lakes and Ponds**

Write words that will help you remember what you learned.

**What Are Lakes and Ponds?**

_____
_____
_____
_____

**Kinds of Lakes**

_____
_____
_____
_____

**Life in Lakes and Ponds**

_____
_____
_____
_____

**Part-Time Ponds**

_____
_____
_____
_____

**Fun at Lakes and Ponds**

_____
_____
_____

## What Are Lakes and Ponds?

**1**. What is the difference between lakes and ponds?

ⓐ their size

ⓑ their shape

ⓒ the land around them

**2**. What are lakes and ponds?

_____

_____

_____

## Kinds of Lakes

**1**. Why do some lakes have salt water?

ⓐ People made dams on them.

ⓑ Lots of salt fell into them.

ⓒ They were part of oceans.

**2**. Tell about one way lakes have formed.

_____

_____

_____

**Lakes and Ponds**

## Life in Lakes and Ponds

1. This reading is MAINLY about ___

   Ⓐ birds that fly to warm places in the fall.

   Ⓑ things that live in or near lakes and ponds.

   Ⓒ animals that are too small to see.

2. Name two kinds of foods birds eat in lakes and ponds.

_____

_____

_____

## Part-Time Ponds

1. How do some part-time ponds form?

   Ⓐ Ponds dry up and form lakes.

   Ⓑ Frogs dig them in the ground.

   Ⓒ Melting snow fills a hole with water.

2. How do frogs live in part-time ponds?

_____

_____

_____

## Fun at Lakes and Ponds

1. "Fun at Lakes and Ponds" is MAINLY about ___

   (A) boats that ride on lakes and ponds.

   (B) how people catch fish in lakes and ponds.

   (C) some ways people use lakes and ponds.

2. Tell about two ways people have fun at lakes and ponds.

_____

_____

_____

## Connect Your Ideas

1. Tell about two ways people use lakes and ponds.

_____

_____

_____

2. Tell about two ways animals use lakes and ponds.

_____

_____

_____

# Reading Log • Level A • Book 2

| | I Read This | New Words I Learned | New Facts I Learned | What Else I Want to Learn About This Subject |
|---|---|---|---|---|
| **How Things Are Measured** | | | | |
| Measuring Earth | | | | |
| Tools for Measuring | | | | |
| Using a Ruler | | | | |
| Long, Wide, and High | | | | |
| Time | | | | |
| **Seasons** | | | | |
| Earth's Tilt | | | | |
| Spring | | | | |
| Summer | | | | |
| Fall | | | | |
| Winter | | | | |
| **Stars** | | | | |
| What Is a Star? | | | | |
| Stars of Different Colors | | | | |
| Stars at Night | | | | |
| Star Patterns | | | | |
| Shooting Stars | | | | |

# Reading Log • Level A • Book 2

| | I Read This | | | | | New Words I Learned | New Facts I Learned | What Else I Want to Learn About This Subject |
|---|---|---|---|---|---|---|---|---|
| **Houses Around the World** | | | | | | | | |
| What Is a House? | | | | | | | | |
| Houses of Ice | | | | | | | | |
| Houses on Stilts | | | | | | | | |
| Houses on the Go | | | | | | | | |
| Houses in the City | | | | | | | | |
| **Places People Work** | | | | | | | | |
| Outdoor Jobs | | | | | | | | |
| Office Jobs | | | | | | | | |
| Store Jobs | | | | | | | | |
| Travel Jobs | | | | | | | | |
| Jobs at Home | | | | | | | | |
| **Lakes and Ponds** | | | | | | | | |
| What Are Lakes and Ponds? | | | | | | | | |
| Kinds of Lakes | | | | | | | | |
| Life in Lakes and Ponds | | | | | | | | |
| Part-Time Ponds | | | | | | | | |
| Fun at Lakes and Ponds | | | | | | | | |

# Self-Check Graph

| | Measuring Earth | Tools for Measuring | Using a Ruler | Long, Wide, and High | Time | Earth's Tilt | Spring | Summer | Fall | Winter | What Is a Star? | Stars of Different Colors | Stars at Night | Star Patterns | Shooting Stars | What Is a House? | Houses of Ice | Houses on Stilts | Houses on the Go | Houses in the City | Outdoor Jobs | Office Jobs | Store Jobs | Travel Jobs | Jobs at Home | What Are Lakes and Ponds? | Kinds of Lakes | Life in Lakes and Ponds | Part-Time Ponds | Fun at Lakes and Ponds |
|---|---|---|---|---|---|---|---|---|---|---|---|---|---|---|---|---|---|---|---|---|---|---|---|---|---|---|---|---|---|---|
| 130 | | | | | | | | | | | | | | | | | | | | | | | | | | | | | | |
| 128 | | | | | | | | | | | | | | | | | | | | | | | | | | | | | | |
| 126 | | | | | | | | | | | | | | | | | | | | | | | | | | | | | | |
| 124 | | | | | | | | | | | | | | | | | | | | | | | | | | | | | | |
| 122 | | | | | | | | | | | | | | | | | | | | | | | | | | | | | | |
| 120 | | | | | | | | | | | | | | | | | | | | | | | | | | | | | | |
| 118 | | | | | | | | | | | | | | | | | | | | | | | | | | | | | | |
| 116 | | | | | | | | | | | | | | | | | | | | | | | | | | | | | | |
| 114 | | | | | | | | | | | | | | | | | | | | | | | | | | | | | | |
| 112 | | | | | | | | | | | | | | | | | | | | | | | | | | | | | | |
| 110 | | | | | | | | | | | | | | | | | | | | | | | | | | | | | | |
| 108 | | | | | | | | | | | | | | | | | | | | | | | | | | | | | | |
| 106 | | | | | | | | | | | | | | | | | | | | | | | | | | | | | | |
| 104 | | | | | | | | | | | | | | | | | | | | | | | | | | | | | | |
| 102 | | | | | | | | | | | | | | | | | | | | | | | | | | | | | | |
| 100 | | | | | | | | | | | | | | | | | | | | | | | | | | | | | | |
| 98 | | | | | | | | | | | | | | | | | | | | | | | | | | | | | | |
| 96 | | | | | | | | | | | | | | | | | | | | | | | | | | | | | | |
| 94 | | | | | | | | | | | | | | | | | | | | | | | | | | | | | | |
| 92 | | | | | | | | | | | | | | | | | | | | | | | | | | | | | | |
| 90 | | | | | | | | | | | | | | | | | | | | | | | | | | | | | | |
| 88 | | | | | | | | | | | | | | | | | | | | | | | | | | | | | | |
| 86 | | | | | | | | | | | | | | | | | | | | | | | | | | | | | | |
| 84 | | | | | | | | | | | | | | | | | | | | | | | | | | | | | | |
| 82 | | | | | | | | | | | | | | | | | | | | | | | | | | | | | | |
| 80 | | | | | | | | | | | | | | | | | | | | | | | | | | | | | | |
| 78 | | | | | | | | | | | | | | | | | | | | | | | | | | | | | | |
| 76 | | | | | | | | | | | | | | | | | | | | | | | | | | | | | | |
| 74 | | | | | | | | | | | | | | | | | | | | | | | | | | | | | | |
| 72 | | | | | | | | | | | | | | | | | | | | | | | | | | | | | | |
| 70 | | | | | | | | | | | | | | | | | | | | | | | | | | | | | | |
| 68 | | | | | | | | | | | | | | | | | | | | | | | | | | | | | | |
| 66 | | | | | | | | | | | | | | | | | | | | | | | | | | | | | | |
| 64 | | | | | | | | | | | | | | | | | | | | | | | | | | | | | | |
| 62 | | | | | | | | | | | | | | | | | | | | | | | | | | | | | | |
| 60 | | | | | | | | | | | | | | | | | | | | | | | | | | | | | | |
| 58 | | | | | | | | | | | | | | | | | | | | | | | | | | | | | | |
| 56 | | | | | | | | | | | | | | | | | | | | | | | | | | | | | | |
| 54 | | | | | | | | | | | | | | | | | | | | | | | | | | | | | | |
| 52 | | | | | | | | | | | | | | | | | | | | | | | | | | | | | | |
| 50 | | | | | | | | | | | | | | | | | | | | | | | | | | | | | | |